Improving Business Processes

Pocket Mentor Series

The Pocket Mentor Series offers immediate solutions to common challenges managers face on the job every day. Each book in the series is packed with handy tools, self-tests, and real-life examples to help you identify your strengths and weaknesses and hone critical skills. Whether you're at your desk, in a meeting, or on the road, these portable guides enable you to tackle the daily demands of your work with greater speed, savvy, and effectiveness.

Books in the series:

Improving Business Processes

Expert Solutions to Everyday Challenges

Harvard Business Review Press

Boston, Massachusetts

Library of Congress Cataloging-in-Publication Data

Improving business processes : expert solutions to everyday challenges.
    p. cm. — (Pocket mentor series)
Includes bibliographical references.
ISBN 978-1-4221-2973-9 (pbk. : alk. paper)   1. Reengineering (Management)
2. Organizational change.   I. Harvard Business School. Press.
HD58.87.I54 2010
658.4'06—dc22

                                                            2010004501

Contents

Improving Business Processes: The Basics

What Are Business Processes?   3

What Is Business Process Improvement?   11

Phase 1: Plan a Business Process Improvement   19

Phase 5: Implement Your Redesigned Business Process   57

Recommendations for putting your improved process to work.

Understanding implementation obstacles   58

Rolling out the new business process   62

Phase 6: Continually Improve Your Business Process   65

Ideas for making your process even better in the future.

Measure the business process's performance   66

Take needed action to improve performance   69

Revise performance metrics and targets as needed   69

Tips and Tools

Tools for Improving Business Processes   73

Worksheets for deciding whether a process improvement is necessary, planning a process redesign, creating a functional activity flowchart, developing a process report card, and benchmarking a process.

Test Yourself   83

A helpful review of concepts presented in this guide. Take it before and after you've read the guide, to see how much you've learned.

Answers to test questions   86

Mentor's Message: Why Improve Your Business Processes?

Your organization's success hinges in large part on how well it carries out its business processes—activities that turn inputs such as knowledge and raw materials into products and services that create value for customers. Every time you improve your company's business processes, you generate crucial benefits for your organization in the form of cost savings, efficiency gains, and greater customer loyalty and profitability.

In this book, you'll discover the key elements of process improvement. You'll start by learning more about the nature of business processes and the benefits of process improvement. You'll gain familiarity with the defining characteristics of a process improvement effort. And you'll find suggestions and strategies for implementing a process improvement project, including planning the project, analyzing an existing process, redesigning the process, acquiring resources to implement your new process design, putting the redesigned process into action, and monitoring and constantly improving the new process.

Even small improvements to a relatively simple process can pay big dividends for your organization. Master the basics of business process improvement, and you'll help sharpen your company's competitive edge and position your business for sustained success.

Mark McDonald, Mentor

Mark McDonald, PhD, is a leading researcher and practitioner of business process design and business architecture. Currently Head of Research for Gartner Executive Programs, he was formerly a partner at Accenture, where he was responsible for directing the firm's Center for Process Excellence. He has worked on several global process transformation initiatives, and is the author of business process reengineering methodology, tools, and proven practices. Mark has written numerous articles on process design and development and is the coauthor with Peter Keen of *The eProcess Edge,* published by McGraw-Hill in 2000.

Improving Business Processes: The Basics

What Are Business Processes?

As a manager, you probably hear extensive discussion of "business process improvement," "process redesign," and "business process reengineering" in your organization. You may wonder what, exactly, these terms mean.

First, it's helpful to understand what business processes are. Below, we offer several useful explanations.

Inputs, activities, and outputs

Technically, a business process is the set of steps a business performs to create value for customers. A process consists of three basic components:

- **Inputs:** They start the process. For example, if you're building a bicycle, the inputs are the tires, wheels, nuts, bolts, chains, gears, and so forth.

- **Activities:** These transform inputs into outputs. In the bicycle example, activities would include building a frame, attaching the wheels, and tuning the gears.

- **Outputs:** Sometimes also called outcomes, outputs are the results of the activities—in this example, the finished bicycles.

Processes are easier to understand when you consider physical goods like bicycles. But processes exist in *every* company—not just those that make physical goods. For instance, in a company that provides management consulting services, there are still inputs (such as a consultant's knowledge), activities (for example, conducting an employee-morale survey at a client organization), and outputs (such as a plan for a cultural-change initiative at the client organization).

People, technology, and information

You can also think of business processes as the series of events that bring together *people*, *technology*, and *information* in ways that create valuable outputs. To do this, take a moment to glance around your office. Notice that:

- The *people* around you are carrying out process *activities* based on the *inputs* they receive—such as customer requests. Their skills and knowledge constitute additional inputs.

- These people are often working with *technology*—for example, software applications and the Internet. These technologies facilitate process *activities*—such as e-mailing a customer or retrieving customer data.

- *Information* is also all around you—stored in databases, provided by customers, or held in people's minds. As such, information can be a process *input* (such as the number of parts in a warehouse) *or* an *output* (for instance, a consultant's report).

In short, business processes constitute all the activities your company engages in—using people, technology, and information—

to carry out its mission, set goals, measure performance, serve customers, and address the inevitable challenges that arise while doing so. Processes determine the effectiveness and efficiency of your company's operations, the quality of your customers' experience—and, ultimately, your organization's financial success.

Every organization contains a large number of business processes. Some are simple processes carried out in a single department—such as entering a customer's order into a computer. Others are complex processes implemented throughout your company—for instance, developing successful products.

Formal and informal processes Processes can also vary in their degree of formality. Here's an example of an *informal* process: Your contact at a company that is a long-time customer asks you for a discount if the company purchases double the normal amount of your product. There is no rule saying you can't provide such a discount, nor is there an established way to give the discount. So you give the discount. You have just created an informal process. Your company hasn't documented this process as a set of steps that must be performed under certain conditions. For now at least, the discount program exists only in your head.

Here's an example of a *formal* process: You manage a call center that resolves customer concerns over the phone and through the Internet. You and your team have established a rigorous set of procedures for answering customers' questions and solving their problems. Your team has documented these procedures, and all new employees are required to study them and receive training before staffing the call center's phones. Thus, the processes for handling customer concerns are highly formalized.

Some processes start out as informal, and then the organization decides to formalize them. For instance, suppose you created an informal process by asking current employees to suggest job candidates for an open position. The process proves highly successful, enabling you to identify and recruit a new hire who then excels on the job. As a result of this success, your company decides to make this practice a formal part of its recruitment efforts. It even sets up a bonus program to reward employees who recommend candidates who are hired.

Process problems Everyone in and related to your organization—you, your boss, peers, and direct reports, and your customers and suppliers—carries out many different processes every day. But because business processes are invisible, many people don't consciously think about them or realize the impact they have on an organization's performance. Instead, when problems do crop up (for example, a customer's order is filled incorrectly), people often look for someone to blame. Managers may spend time and money replacing the person supposedly at fault. Or they might choose to invest in expensive new technology to try to overcome the problem.

Yet many managers find that these "solutions" don't work. Ultimately, the same problems keep surfacing. What's going on? As it turns out, most organizational difficulties stem from flawed processes—not incompetent individuals or inadequate technology. By understanding the process glitches that led to a problem, you and your team can correct the process to get the results your company wants.

> *Don't find fault, find a remedy.*
> —Henry Ford

The need for a process mindset   Because establishing the right business processes is so essential to an organization's survival, you and your team can create enormous value for your company by adopting a *process mindset*. When you have a process mindset, you regularly think about how to improve the way your group turns inputs into desired outputs. You seek to understand the quality of your group's business processes by using measurements and process mapping to discover and correct weak points.

You can cultivate a process mindset in your team by helping team members understand and articulate the many business processes they take part in, and by encouraging them to constantly look for ways to *improve* those processes. Your reward? Greater efficiency, higher customer satisfaction, reduced errors, lower costs, and enhanced company profitability.

See "Tips for developing a process mindset in your team" for more information.

Tips for developing a process mindset in your team

- Help your employees understand that the team's work is composed of tasks that result in an output. The way these tasks are put together is a process. Each person in the team is part of one or more business processes.
- Ask people involved in a process to map the steps in the process. Ask them to identify the inputs and outputs for each step. Consider using sticky notes of different shapes and colors to build the map.

- Invite people to specify the inputs necessary for their work, to describe the work they do, and to identify the outputs. Ask them, "Who receives your outputs? What do they do with the outputs? How does the quality of your outputs affect their job?"
- Make a distinction between core and support processes. Core processes deliver value to customers directly; for example, customer support and product development. Support processes enable core processes and include hiring and training, budget approvals, purchasing, and other everyday operations.
- Have "upstream" workers interview "downstream" workers to see how upstream work affects downstream work. For example, order-entry people could question customer-fulfillment people to determine how unclear specifications and lack of customer information affects the processing of orders.
- Create a flow chart of the processes in your team. Then explore with your team what happens when variations—accommodating last-minute requests, not following established communication steps—are introduced into the process. Consider how workers and customers are affected when people don't follow established processes.

What Is Business Process Improvement?

ow that you know more about what business processes are, let's look closely look at the many dimensions of business process improvement, or BPI.

A definition

Business process improvement (BPI) is a set of disciplined approaches and tools that managers use to enhance their company's performance. As the name suggests, BPI (also called business process management, or BPM) focuses on changing business processes to improve their effectiveness. In organizations that use BPI:

- Managers and employees know their business processes and capture them in process maps, procedure manuals, or agreed-upon "ways of doing things."

- Managers track the performance of processes in the form of metrics that can assess the quality of inputs and outputs or gauge the effectiveness of activities.

- Top management systematically invests in its processes. In some cases, these investments are intended to improve current operations—for example, enhancing the efficiency of order processing. In other cases, these investments are meant to improve the company's competitive position—for instance, strengthening the product-development or strategy-formulation process.

- Organizations that do not use BPI may do these same things. However, their use of BPI is usually sporadic, rather than a regular way of doing business.

BPI is a tool that can be used at every level of an organization—by a manager who sets out to change a relatively simple process within her department or by top executives who introduce a companywide initiative designed to improve performance throughout the organization.

Formal BPI methodologies and standards

This book focuses on BPI efforts that you can initiate and carry out in your own team or department. However, your organization may also have mandated a large-scale process improvement program in which all managers are required to participate. If that's the case, you may want to briefly familiarize yourself with some of those programs. The table "Formal Process Improvement Methodologies and Standards" shows examples.

Triggers for a BPI effort

A BPI effort can be triggered by several types of events. These include inefficiencies or problematic performance. For instance, Kara, a manager at a regional sales office for a large consumer-goods company, realizes that the office's sales figures are 5 percent lower than those of other regional offices. Her staff work hard, but

What Would YOU Do?

Flat Results at Pedal Power

P AUL RECENTLY BECAME manager of Pedal Power, a
bicycle tour guide company. Nine months earlier, the
company had established a new service: sending e-mails to customers notifying them of tour updates and inviting them to down-
load the latest tours and travel information.

Customers initially expressed delight with the service. But in
the past month, many customers have complained that the travel
information they received in the e-mails was out of date. Paul realizes that something is wrong with the content-updating and distri-
bution process he uses for the e-mails. But he's unsure how to
address the problem.

What would YOU do? The mentor will suggest a solution in
What You COULD Do.

---

they're not achieving their goals. Kara decides to examine key
processes—such as the way her staff qualifies sales leads and sets
up customer accounts—to see whether any of these processes
could be changed in order to increase the sales figures.

Major changes in the business landscape can also trigger a BPI
effort. Business change can take many forms—including new

TABLE 1

Formal process improvement methodologies and standards

Name	Description
Six Sigma	Disciplined, data-driven methodology for eliminating defects in any process, designed to deliver high performance, reliability, and customer value. Motorola developed Six Sigma in the 1980s after recognizing that products with the fewest defects failed least often during use. The Greek letter *sigma* denotes variation from a standard.
Total Quality Management (TQM)	Management strategy aimed at embedding awareness of quality in all organizational processes and encouraging employees to steadily increase customer satisfaction at continually lower costs. TQM was popularized in Japan after World War II by American statistician and college professor W. Edwards Deming. Later, Joseph Juran broadened the concept of quality management from its statistical origins to focus on the human dimension.
ISO 9000	Family of standards for quality management systems from the International Organization for Standardization (ISO). These standards do not guarantee the quality of end products and services; rather, they certify that a company is applying consistent business processes. ISO 9000 standards are administered by accreditation and certification bodies.
Business Process Reengineering (BPR)	Management approach that promoted radical redesign of workflow within and between enterprises in order to achieve dramatic performance improvement. BPR reached its heyday in the early 1990s, when Michael Hammer and James Champy published their best-selling book, *Reengineering the Corporation*.

technologies, shifts in customer preferences, and the emergence of new competitors. For example, Marcus, a manager in his company's human resources department, is intrigued by the possibilities the Internet presents. He realizes that providing the means for employees to make their yearly benefits changes online would help the company save time and money. Previously, employees who wanted to change their benefits choices had to meet with HR personnel—a time-consuming, and therefore costly, process. Marcus sets out to review the way the HR department currently carries out its work and to develop ideas for using the Internet to introduce new efficiency to as many processes as possible.

Benefits of BPI

A well-run BPI initiative enables you to generate many important results for your organization. For instance, BPI could help you understand how effectively your team is meeting the needs of customers and other departments in your company. It could aid you in revising your hiring strategies to improve skill levels and expertise in your team. It could save your company time and money by simplifying overly complex and expensive processes. And it could help you identify entirely new processes that enable your firm to provide top-notch customer service while reducing costs.

The six phases of BPI

BPI offers crucial benefits to any team or organization. But to generate those benefits, you need to take a structured approach to your process improvement efforts. Experts recommend the following six phases for relatively complex process improvements:

1. **Plan:** Select an existing business process you want to improve, define its scope, and assemble your team.

2. **Analyze:** Closely examine the process you've identified as a candidate for improvement.

3. **Redesign:** Determine what changes you want to make to the target process.

4. **Acquire resources:** Obtain the personnel, equipment, and other resources needed to make the process changes called for in your redesign.

5. **Implement:** Carry out the process changes.

6. **Continually improve:** Constantly evaluate the target process's effectiveness and make further changes as necessary.

Of course, when you make *simple* process improvements in your department, you won't necessarily take the time to carry out each of the six phases explicitly. Rather, you'll likely think through the phases quickly. For example, suppose you want to make your team's decision-making process more efficient. Currently, you gather input from each team member personally during the week before making a key decision. But with the addition of several new hires, this process has become unwieldy and time-consuming. You envision and suggest a change: Instead of the current process, employees will start meeting once a week to discuss key issues. The team makes the shift—freeing up more of your time, which you then invest in other responsibilities.

What You COULD Do.

Remember Paul's worry about Pedal Power's problematic e-mail updates?

Here's what the mentor suggests:

Although Paul's process is virtual, he can envision it much like a traditional manufacturing process. This will help him begin implementation of a business process improvement (BPI) initiative. His next step is to assemble a BPI team to analyze the existing process. The team will then redesign the process to eliminate problems. Next, the team will have to acquire the resources needed to implement the new process (such as personnel or equipment). Paul's team might then pilot the new process to address any remaining problems before putting it to full use. Even after the new process has become standard operating procedure, the BPI team will continue to monitor its performance and make further improvements as needed.

Phase 1: Plan a Business Process Improvement

To plan a business process improvement, take the following steps:

- Detect signs of trouble

- Select a process to improve

- Define the BPI's scope, goals, and schedule

- Assemble your BPI team

- Get everyone on board

We'll look at each of these steps in the pages below.

Detect signs of trouble

To plan a business process improvement, first decide whether process improvement is needed. The answer is yes if you notice certain telltale symptoms—including the following:

- Customers are increasingly commenting that your company's product has deteriorated.

- Certain procedures seem overly complicated.

- Tasks take longer to complete than they did previously, or there is noticeable variation in the amount of time different people take to perform the same task.

- Things don't get done right the first time.

- Your team's performance is declining, or the team is consistently failing to reach agreed-upon goals.

- Employees are expressing frustration over confusing processes or bottlenecks that prevent them from fulfilling their job responsibilities.

> *In life, as in chess, forethought wins.*
> —Charles Buxton

Select a process to improve

If you're like most managers, you may see several symptoms of problematic processes occurring simultaneously. This suggests that more than one process may benefit from improvement. For example, Joe, who manages a regional office for a financial services company, has noticed that customers are complaining about having to provide the same personal information several times while applying for a loan. In addition, the office's growth—in terms of the number of new accounts signed per quarter—is lower than that of other regions, despite the considerable expertise of Joe's staff.

When it seems that several processes may need improvement, how do you decide which one to tackle first? Create a *process selection matrix* in which you rate each process according to criteria such as how easily it might be changed and how problematic it may be for customers. Rate each possibly problematic process on a scale of 1 to 5, with 5 being the highest score and 1 the lowest. The table "Joe's process selection matrix" shows an example.

TABLE 2

Joe's process selection matrix

Process	Cost-saving potential	Source of customer complaints	Opportunity for improvement	Easy to change	Source of staff frustration	Total score
Setting up new accounts	5	5	2	2	4	18
Evaluating applicants' credit histories	4	2	4	3	4	17
Approving loan applications	4	1	3	2	4	14

Tips for prioritizing business process improvement efforts

- Determine which process in your team is most critical to your team's ability to contribute to the organization. Ask team members, as well as external stakeholders such as vendors and customers, for their point of view.
- Prioritize processes that have the greatest impact on customers.
- Select processes for improvement that will generate the most benefit for the least amount of investment.

- Look for processes that result in costly problems—such as failure to meet customer needs, high costs, or long cycle times.
- Identify processes needing improvement based on internal considerations. For example, a problematic process is causing unnecessary conflict among team members, preventing them from concentrating on meeting customers' needs.

Once you've rated each process, total up your scores. The highest score suggests the process you might want to improve first. In Joe's case, he decides to focus on the process of setting up new accounts.

See "Tips for prioritizing business process improvement efforts" for more information.

Define the BPI's scope, goals, and schedule

Define the scope, goals, and schedule for the selected process improvement project. *Scope* defines what will and won't be included in the effort. For example, to improve the way his office sets up new accounts, Joe decides to focus on changing the way people and technology interact to establish accounts. He prefers not to change people's jobs or adopt new technologies if he can help it.

Also specify how the BPI effort supports your organization's *goals*. Clarify how it relates to other existing processes, as well as to important stakeholders, such as your company's customers or suppliers. And express the desired improvement in numerical terms. Joe, for instance, determines that improving how his office sets up new accounts will help his company achieve its strategic goal of serving customers more efficiently and quickly. The process of setting up accounts directly affects customers' satisfaction levels and has links to the other processes involved in approving loan applications, such as evaluating applicants' credit histories. Joe expresses the desired improvement as: "Customers have to provide financial information only once in order to establish an account with us."

To define *schedule*, specify which milestones you'll need to achieve in order to change the problematic process and approximately when you expect to reach each milestone. For example, Joe's BPI milestones include mapping the current new-account process within two months and conducting a trial run of a revised process by the end of the third quarter.

Assemble your BPI team

Decide who will carry out the BPI project. Your team should include the following:

- **Project manager:** Select someone to serve as project manager—whether it's yourself or another individual. The project manager should have experience working with others on focused tasks. He or she will be responsible for ensuring that the work gets done on time, all issues are resolved, and the project achieves its goals.

- **Process owner:** The process owner will take responsibility for continually improving the process once the BPI team redesigns it. Again, this may be you. He or she should be thoroughly familiar with the redesigned process, open to making further changes to it as needed, and able to influence others to accept changes. The process owner also needs to understand the principles of effective process design, be able to track the new process's performance using metrics, and maintain documents related to the process (such as flow charts, standard operating procedures, and checklists).

- **Process users:** Include individuals who work directly with the process. Select a representative sample, not just the people who perform the process the best.

- **Skeptics:** BPI teams also benefit from one or more skeptics— people who will challenge the design process and stimulate productive debate over ideas.

- **Facilitator:** If your BPI project is extensive, consider including a facilitation specialist—someone with expertise in leading team meetings. Often, the project manager can fill this role.

- **Technology expert:** Technology plays a role in most processes. Thus, having access to a technology expert—for example, your company's Web-site administrator or technical support analyst—can be valuable.

Get everyone on board

Establish ground rules for how the BPI team members will work together. For instance, how often will you meet to discuss progress and address challenges? Who will be responsible for which aspects of the work? How will team members share information and resolve conflicts?

If necessary, gain your own manager's commitment to the BPI initiative by making a compelling business case for the value of the project. Finally, decide with your manager when and how the BPI team will provide updates on its progress.

Phase 2: Analyze the Existing Business Process

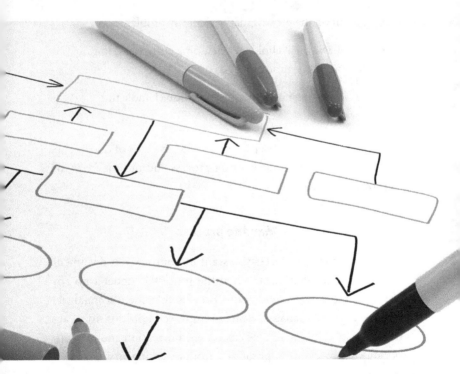

N ow that you've planned your BPI project, it's time to move to phase two—analyzing the process you've identified as needing change. This phase consists of the following steps:

- Mapping the existing process (documenting the way work flows through the process).

- Examining the process map to identify problems.

- Interviewing stakeholders (including customers) to gain their insights on the process.

- Benchmarking how other organizations handle this process.

After following these steps, you should have a set of documents that precisely describe the existing process and include ideas for improving the process.

Map the process

When you map the process you want to improve, you document all the activities that occur when the process is under way. For example, the new-account setup process that Joe, the financial services regional manager, wants to improve might consist of activities such as taking in new customer information and loan applications; processing applications, from accepting an application through rendering a decision; and sending loan applications to the credit department for risk analysis and approval.

To document the current process's steps, gather data on all aspects of the process—such as how many transactions are involved during one cycle of the process, how often the process takes place, and so forth.

Then use the information you've collected to create a map, or an "as is" flowchart, of the process. Flowcharts use specific symbols to convey precise information. Figure 1 defines the symbols; look to the maps that follow for examples of how to use them.

FIGURE 1

Flowchart symbols

Symbol	Example	Meaning
Box	Take order	An activity that a person or technology performs
Diamond	Does it make criterion?	A review or decision that a person or technology must conduct or make
Arrow	→	The direction of the work flow; arrows can appear between any flowchart symbols
Triangle	Store documents	Filing or storage of materials or information

(continued)

FIGURE 1 (continued)

Flowchart symbols

Big D	Waiting in queue	A delay, such as batching, bottlenecking, equipment breakdowns, or time spent waiting for information
Oval	Stop	The beginning and end of a process map
Circle	See map A	A cross-reference to another process

Create two versions of your "as is" flowchart:

- **Macro flowchart:** A macro flowchart typically depicts the 2 to 7 steps that make up the process's *critical* elements.

FIGURE 2

Macro flowchart

- **Functional activity flowchart:** This version of your "as is" flowchart depicts the more detailed steps in the process, as well as the job titles of people working in the process and the activities performed by each individual.

The following is an "as is" functional activity flowchart of Joe's new-account setup process:

FIGURE 3

An "as is" flowchart

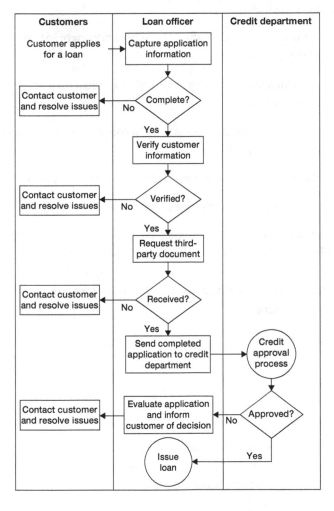

Examine the map for problems

Examine each component of your process map, asking yourself questions such as:

- At which points does this process break down or experience delays?

- At which points do people typically experience frustration with the process?

- Which parts of the process seem to consume an inordinate amount of time?

- Which parts of the process lead to low-quality outcomes?

- Which parts of the process incur unacceptable costs?

For example, after examining his process map, a manager might conclude that his team could save time by automating parts of his process to increase efficiency and employee satisfaction.

See "Steps for creating a functional activity flowchart" for additional suggestions.

Steps for creating a functional activity flowchart

1. **Define the process boundaries.** With your business process improvement team, identify the activities or decisions that mark the process's beginning and end.

2. **Document the job titles of people involved in the process.** On the left-hand side of a piece of paper, list the job titles of all the people who work in the process.

3. **Create "swim lanes."** Separate the job titles with horizontal or vertical lines. These become "swim lanes," which enable you to follow the work of individuals, see where handoffs occur, and identify imbalances of work among participants in the process.

4. **Add process details.** For each job title in your chart, insert a box representing what that person does in the process. Inside the box, use verb-noun combinations to describe what that person does. For example, "Receive application" or "Set up file." Insert diamonds representing decisions people must make while carrying out the process. Inside the diamonds, use questions to represent the decisions. For example, "Is file complete?" or "Was log-out OK?"

5. **Show the sequence of activities.** Number each box and diamond in your flowchart to indicate the sequence in which activities are carried out during the process. Ensure that each box and diamond has a unique number.

Interview stakeholders

Meet with stakeholders in the process—people who are affected by it, care about it, or work in it. Stakeholders might include your supervisor, peer managers, employees, and even customers and suppliers. Ask them how they view the process and what they think works well and not so well in the process. Invite them to offer suggestions for improvement.

For instance, after examining his map of the new-account setup process, Joe had concluded that his team could save time by gathering all customer documentation at the moment the application is received, rather than going back to the customer to ask for it later. He also realized that the process contains multiple decision points where a person must evaluate a loan's progress and possibly take corrective action. This can introduce errors and delays in serving customers.

Joe sets out to interview stakeholders. Through talking with the loan officers, Joe finds that they spend much of their time coordinating document flows between the customer and the credit department. He learns that customers rarely bring all the information needed to complete a loan (such as proof of income) to their initial visit. Thus loan officers must track down this information to process the loan.

In interviewing stakeholders, don't forget to ask customers what they want from the process. Then fill out a report indicating how they would "grade" your team on each requirement and what "A" level performance would look like—to them—for each.

For example, Joe's customers want to provide information only once while applying for a loan (their idea of "A" level performance on this requirement). Perhaps they would give this requirement a "C" grade because of their frustration with having to provide information several times.

Benchmark

In addition to interviewing stakeholders, find out how other organizations conduct the process you want to redesign. These other organizations can include competitors, companies that are similar to yours but that don't compete directly, and enterprises that are considered "world class" in your target process. Your goal in benchmarking is to generate additional ideas for redesigning the problematic process.

To generate ideas for which organizations you might benchmark, use sources such as research companies, consultancies, industry studies, industry trade associations, and former employees of competitors. You can also contact organizations yourself and conduct brief interviews with managers and executives about how their company carries out the process in question.

See "Tips for benchmarking and researching the best business processes" for additional information.

Tips for benchmarking and researching the best business processes

- Examine how the process you want to improve is performed by direct competitors, organizations that are in your industry but not direct competitors, and world-class organizations regardless of industry. Divide your business process improvement (BPI) team into three groups, and assign one benchmarking category to each group.

- To benchmark how industry competitors perform the process in question, consider the following sources of information: industry trade associations that conduct benchmarking studies, accounting and consulting firms that specialize in your industry, distributors that handle competitors' products, former employees of rival companies, public documents published by competitors (such as annual reports and press packages), rival companies' customers and suppliers.

- Prepare a list of questions to present to people you interview. Your list may include questions such as "How have you eliminated points in this process where employees experience frustration?" and "How do you currently prevent bottlenecks in this process?"
- Prepare a script with which members of your BPI team will introduce themselves to benchmarking interviewees before presenting them with questions.

Phase 3: Redesign Your Business Process

You've analyzed the existing process that you identified for improvement. Now it's time for your BPI team to redesign the process so that it produces the outcomes you're looking for. The redesign phase consists of these steps:

- Envisioning a better process

- Testing your team's ideas

- Considering the implications of a potential redesign

- Documenting your redesign

- Gathering feedback from stakeholders and refining the redesigned process

At the end of your redesign phase, you should have a set of documents describing the proposed process redesign that is approved by management and other key stakeholders.

Envision a better process

With the rest of the BPI team, visualize what an ideal process would look like. Be sure that the ideal process directly addresses the business problem or opportunity identified in the project goals. Drawing on your stakeholder interviews, benchmarking, and other activities from the analysis phase, brainstorm ways to make the process better.

During this brainstorming, set aside the "as is" process flow-chart, so new ideas won't be influenced by the status quo. Then think about ways to improve the process's performance. First, think about ways to *exceed customers' expectations*. Could the accuracy, speed, and quality of the process be improved? How might the process be improved to make it easier for customers to do business with the company?

Second, consider ways to *cut costs*. Could steps be eliminated from the process to reduce the number of resources required or reduce the cost of the resources used? Third, brainstorm ideas for *reducing cycle time*—the total time it takes to complete the process. Could requests for clarification or information be eliminated to speed up the process?

In addition to brainstorming ways to improve the process, determine how to measure the new process's performance. Define performance metrics related to:

- **Customer satisfaction**—for example, "Number of times customer has to phone the company before getting their problem solved" or "Amount of time on hold."

- **Quality**—such as "Number of errors in assembly."

- **Cost**—such as "Amount spent per quarter on parts."

- **Cycle time**—for instance, "Number of hours to assemble one unit of a product."

Joe's BPI team came up with several ideas for a better process, including the following:

- **Ask for documentation up front.** Currently, customer information is verified late in the process. For example, the customer is asked to provide proof of income after the loan application is accepted, creating a one- to three-day delay in the process and requiring the loan officer to contact the applicant. A review of the process's history revealed that this step was originally included to avoid having the credit department work on an application only to find out that the applicant did not meet the required income criteria. However, because fewer than 3 percent of loan applications are rejected, the new process should ask borrowers to submit their proof of income at the time they make the application. This would accelerate the process and eliminate the expense of the loan officer following up to request documentation.

- **Add a new staff position.** Loan officers are responsible for managing the loan-application cycle, including ensuring that the right documentation is gathered and processed. Therefore, loan officers have to follow up on any questions and outstanding issues. This step was intended to ensure that customers received personal service from loan officers. However, it limits the number of loans an officer can handle at any one time, reducing their ability to generate new sales. Creating a loan production coordinator position to handle routine documentation requests would free up loan officers' time and let them generate more new accounts. Loan officer time is costly—not only because loan officers are paid salary and commission, but also because time spent gathering information is time away from generating new business. Adding a loan production coordinator position would save the company money, because the task of contacting customers would now be performed by a person in an administrative position.

See "Steps for envisioning a better business process" for additional ideas.

Steps for envisioning a better business process

1. **Write stories describing the ideal process.** Have each member of your business process improvement team write a story about how he or she would change the problematic process so that it delights customers, saves time, and/or cuts costs. Team members can create stories from the perspective of a customer, someone working in the process, or someone observing the process from outside. They can also draw on ideas from process benchmarking and best practices.
2. **Read the stories out loud.** Have each person read his or her story to everyone else. As team members listen to the stories, have them jot down the ideas for process redesign that appeal most to them.
3. **Document ideas.** After all the stories have been read, create two lists: process redesign ideas that most team members like, and ideas that require more discussion.

4. **Discuss the ideas.** Discuss ideas until the team reaches a consensus on one redesign. If you can't reach consensus after everyone's ideas and positions have been heard, accept that you will have several design variations at this stage.

Test your team's ideas

Your team may envision several possible new processes that would improve on the current one. After gathering as many ideas as possible, test those proposed processes to determine which of them seems best. Consider these testing mechanisms:

- **Role-playing:** Have team members act out the proposed process to see how well it works. Assign someone to take the role of customer, another to play an order taker, and so on. Create artificial—but realistic—orders, contracts, or requests and ask each person to play his or her role while carrying out the process. Observe how things go: look for bottlenecks, coordination problems, and other difficulties that may disqualify the process as ideal. For instance, in the role play performed by Joe's BPI team, one person plays the customer, filling out an actual loan application form and approaching the bank. A "loan officer" manually checks the application and writes down the information needed to verify and validate the application. The completed application is then handed off to the credit department.

- **Practice:** Start with real inputs—such as orders, contracts or requests—and have the people who would actually be carrying out the real process try turning those inputs into outputs. Again, look for difficulties or surprises that may indicate the proposed process would not work smoothly.

- **Computer simulation:** Many software vendors offer applications that enable managers to test proposed processes under various scenarios to find bottlenecks and other problems. If you have access to such software, consider experimenting with it to evaluate the top processes proposed by your BPI team.

Testing your ideas helps you make corrections during the design process, when they are easy and inexpensive to make. It might also help you find previously unidentified glitches in the process. For example, during Joe's role-play, the loan officer asks the "customer" for documentation. The customer replies: "What documentation? I just gave you an application." Joe realizes that providing customers with a checklist of the documentation they need to supply when applying for a loan would speed up the application process—and would decrease customers' frustration.

Consider a new design's implications

To further gauge the feasibility of your redesigned process, discuss the organizational ramifications of the redesign with your team. Talk about how the new process might affect your company's structures, employees, customers, and systems. The table "Examining a Redesign's Organizational Implications" shows examples. Depending on the nature of your redesign's organizational implications, you may decide that your team's proposed process

TABLE 3

Examining a redesign's organizational implications

Organizational aspect	Will the new process require . . .
Structure	The creation of new jobs, departments, or reporting relationships, or major modifications of existing structures?
Employees	New skills, knowledge, and expertise that must be acquired by training existing employees or hiring new personnel?
Customers	New marketing plans or other communications to inform customers of the redesigned process and to help them use it?
Systems	Entirely new systems—such as a new IT infrastructure—or the significant modification of existing systems?

needs further changes. For example, Joe realizes that creating a loan production coordinator position might tempt the loan officers to care less about the quality of their work. So he decides to create metrics to track which loan officers' applications require the most work to complete, and to make these metrics part of the loan officers' formal performance reviews.

Document your new design

Document the latest version of your redesign in an activity flow-chart. Omit details about who will do which tasks. That information will come later. For now, you want to present a relatively simple version of the process to stakeholders to invite their feedback and ideas.

> *The general who wins the battle makes many calculations in his temple before the battle is fought.*
> —Sun Tzu

Refine the new design

Present the new activity flowchart—along with information about how you generated ideas for the proposed process—to key stakeholders. These stakeholders will likely include your manager as well as others in the company who would be affected by the changed process. Ask stakeholders the following questions:

- "Does this process, as designed, address the performance issues identified in the project goal? Does it enable us to take advantage of important opportunities?"

- "Where do you see potential issues arising in this proposed process?"

- "What suggestions would you offer to improve the process's effectiveness at achieving the project goals?"

- "In your opinion, have we missed something that's important? If so, what is it?"

By inviting contributions from stakeholders, you begin building support for the new process your team has crafted. When people contribute ideas for changing a process, they often feel more committed to it. Consider whether you want to further revise your proposed process to incorporate some of the feedback.

See "Tips for redesigning a business process" for more information.

Tips for redesigning a business process

- Change the process in ways that provide value that the customer wants—for example, more speed and efficiency, more accuracy, less cost, or a single point of contact between customers and your company.
- Don't be constrained by current job titles, responsibilities, and locations. If you need to create a new position to make the process flow as effectively as possible, consider doing so.
- If inputs to your process naturally form a cluster, create a separate process for each cluster.
- Attack the biggest time-wasters in the process first—such as points where there is extensive waiting, moving, or rework.
- Where steps in the process can be done independently of one another, without having to be in a particular sequence, consider creating several processes that can operate in parallel.
- Examine the logic behind the current sequence of steps in the process. Ask yourself whether the process would work more quickly or efficiently if you rearranged the steps.
- Look for opportunities to remove unnecessary reviews of completed work. When people know that their work will be reviewed multiple times, the incentive to get it right the first time diminishes.

- To decrease the number of steps in a process, eliminate signoffs or approvals by individuals on activities they don't know much about. Instead, push decision-making down to where the work is actually being done.
- Identify opportunities to simplify steps that are unnecessarily complex.
- Involve as few people as possible in performing a process. You'll reduce the number of potential bottlenecks and other problems.
- Identify problem points in the process by asking the people involved where they experience frustration, and by asking what, precisely, frustrates them. Answers might include "When this part of the work gets to me, there's missing information."
- To identify bottlenecks in the current process, increase the inputs flowing through it, and accelerate the speed at which the process is performed. Bottlenecks will become more noticeable under these conditions.

Phase 4: Acquire Needed Resources

N ow that your BPI team has created a new design for your problematic process, it's time to identify—and obtain— the resources you'll need to put the redesign into action. Regardless of what business unit you work in, this phase may require you to collaborate with several other units or departments within your organization. If the scope of your proposed process change is large, you will likely work closely with one or more of the following groups:

- Human Resources (HR)

- IT

- Finance

When you finish this phase of your BPI initiative, you should have all the required resources on hand.

Understand resource types

Depending on the complexity and scope of your new process, the resources you'll need can vary dramatically. For example, a process change may require:

- **New or changed work roles.** With many BPI efforts, you may decide to use consultants or contractors to perform the redesigned process. Or you may change an existing employee's job responsibilities so that he or she now performs part of the redesigned process, or hire entirely new employees to carry out the process. For example, a BPI team at SalesCo decides to create a more targeted selling process that requires breaking down the existing sales force into smaller territories. This means that the company must hire several new salespeople for each of the reconfigured territories.

- **New equipment or technology.** Some process redesigns require new equipment or technology. To illustrate, to make its product-design process more efficient, NewBrand has decided that designers need to be able to share their electronic files more easily with marketers and product developers. In addition, designers have to be able to reproduce hard copies of their designs more quickly than before. To support these changes, the company decides to acquire new graphics software and printing equipment.

- **New physical space where equipment and technology can reside or where people can carry out the process.** For instance, the BPI team at NewBrand realizes that the company will need to designate space in the design department for the new printing equipment.

- **Support from information technology experts.** For example, BigCo's new way of segmenting markets and conducting market research requires the addition of customer-relationship management (CRM) software modules to the organization's current customer databases. Several experts

What Would YOU Do?

Extreme Process Improvement at Xtreme Gear

LYNN HEADS A regional sales team at Xtreme Gear, a sporting goods company. She has recently realized that other regional teams are both managing and acquiring more accounts than her people are. In interviewing several of her salespeople to see how they carry out their job responsibilities, she learns that each salesperson manages his or her own calendar, scheduling as many customer visits as possible during the work day. Between visits, they try to phone and e-mail other current and potential customers to schedule future sales calls.

Lynn uses this information to create an "as is" flowchart depicting the process her sales reps employ to book sales calls. The flowchart brings an important problem into sharp focus: The more visits a sales rep makes during the day, the less time he or she has to contact existing and potential accounts to arrange future visits. Less time spent scheduling new sales calls means fewer visits being booked. And fewer visits means fewer accounts acquired and slower growth in new accounts.

Lynn realizes that the process for scheduling sales calls needs redesigning. But she's unsure of how to proceed. Should she show her team members and boss her "as is" flowchart and ask them for ideas on how to improve the process? Challenge her salespeople to imagine an ideal process? Mandate some quick and easy changes that will generate immediate results? Because all these options seem plausible, Lynn's confusion deepens.

What would YOU do? The mentor will suggest a solution in *What You COULD Do*.

from BigCo's IT department will need to step in to ensure that the new software modules work well with the existing databases and to resolve any problems with functionality that may arise.

- **Training.** To illustrate, once BigCo's new CRM modules are in place, the company will need to train marketers and customer-service personnel to use the new technology.

- **New management responsibilities and metrics.** A new process often creates new responsibilities that need to be incorporated into management activities. For instance, a manager in a department that has overhauled a process may want to start evaluating his or her employees' performance according to new criteria related to the redesigned process.

Of course, many process changes are more minor and require less substantial resources. For example, to implement his redesigned process for establishing new accounts, Joe may need people from HR to draft the job description for the new position of loan production coordinator. He may also need someone from IT to help ensure that the loan officers are using the right tools to enter customer information.

Obtain the resources

Once you've identified the resources you'll need to implement your new process, you'll have to figure out how to acquire them. To build the required infrastructure and gather necessary materials, you will likely need to work with other departments or business units. For example, if your redesigned process requires extensive new equipment or technology, you will probably have to order these materials through your company's purchasing or IT department.

If numerous people will require training in using the new process, you may have to work with the human resources department to provide relevant workshops or courses. However, if the redesigned process requires that just one person be trained in a relatively straightforward task that does not call for a change in job responsibilities, you may not need formal HR involvement. In this case, you may be able to simply ask another employee in your department to meet with the employee and explain the new task to him or her.

What You COULD Do.

Remember Lynn's question about how best to improve her team's process for scheduling sales calls?

Here's what the mentor suggests:

Lynn shouldn't show her team and boss the "as is" flowchart: Doing so could cause her and others who see the map to become overly influenced by the status quo. She also shouldn't unilaterally decide how to redesign the sales-call scheduling process, because she might miss out on valuable ideas from the people who regularly work in the process, as well as from other stakeholders.

Lynn's best move would be to set aside the "as is" map and encourage everyone to envision a better process. She can help generate a wide range of ideas in brainstorming sessions by asking people to explore questions such as:

- "How would we *like* this process to work, in an ideal world?"
- "How can we achieve more of our goals?"
- "What could we do to exceed performance expectations?"

Phase 5: Implement Your Redesigned Business Process

With resources in place and the process design completed and tested, you're ready to implement your redesigned process. That is, you'll actually start using the new process within your organization.

Many experts maintain that implementation is the most difficult step in any BPI effort. To boost your chances of success, think of implementation as consisting of these parts:

- Understanding implementation obstacles

- Rolling out the new process

Understanding implementation obstacles

Before implementing your new process, it's useful to understand common obstacles to implementing a redesign and to ask yourself whether you've taken steps to avoid them. The table "Common Implementation Obstacles" shows examples.

You can avoid many implementation obstacles by laying the groundwork early in your BPI effort. For example, help managers and employees see the importance of changing the process, and involve them in the redesign. The more they participate, the more they will understand the value of the change and support its implementation. For instance, asking people to take part in testing the new process will help them see that the change is feasible, and will get them on board for implementation.

TABLE 4

Common implementation obstacles

Obstacle	Explanation and example	Ways to avoid
Resistance from employees	Any process change carries the implicit assumption that people were doing the wrong thing in the old process. So, you can expect some resistance to the new process from employees, particularly if there is no easy way for them to see the benefits of making the change.	Acknowledge employee concerns by pointing out how the new process solves the problems raised by the old process. Help employees see how they will benefit from adopting the new process. And clearly explain any changes in workloads and compensation that will come with the new process.
Resistance from managers	If a redesigned process crosses several departments or units, turf disputes can crop up when it comes time for implementation. Specifically, managers in some units may be unwilling to change the way they work in order to put the new process into action.	This issue needs to be addressed before implementation—during development and testing if possible. Managers need to see that supporting the new process will make their job easier or enable them to deliver better performance.
		To win their support, highlight the business problems that the current process is causing, their performance in the old process, their ability to improve that performance by using the new process, and how the new process will benefit them.

(continued)

TABLE 4 (continued)

Obstacle	Explanation and example	Ways to avoid
No champion to push the effort	Every process change requires a champion— the person who provides executive support to the project. In cases of a major process change, the CEO or a high-level leader may be the champion.	If the project never had a champion, it should not have started in the first place. If the champion has changed or lost interest, however, remind him or her of the business value that the BPI effort will generate.
	The champion provides the executive authority to make changes to the process and to reallocate responsibilities.	Make sure the champion *visibly* demonstrates his or her support for the project to other managers and the employees involved. A memo or e-mail from the champion is not enough. People need to see that the champion will make the tough decisions required to achieve the goals.

See "Tips for overcoming resistance to a redesigned business process" for more information.

Difficulties mastered are opportunities won.

—Winston Churchill

Tips for overcoming resistance to a redesigned business process

- Involve stakeholders (anyone affected by a changed process) in designing any improvement you recommend. People are more likely to support a change they have helped to create.

- Ask stakeholders for their input on your "as is" process flowchart, on your proposed redesign, and during the actual implementation.
- Invite everyone, including those who seem to be resisting the change, to share their opinions on the redesign. Write their concerns on a flip chart, and let them know that your team is aware of their issues. Resisters may have valid points that you need to address in your process redesign.
- When proposing a process redesign, make it clear that the *process* is the problem—not the people who work in that process. Often people who have worked in a particular process for years may identify with how the work is currently done, and may have difficulty agreeing to a change.
- Early in your process redesign effort, acknowledge your appreciation for the accomplishments of the people who have worked in the process in the past. This lets them know there's nothing wrong with their work, making it easier for them to be open to change.
- State the reason for redesigning a problematic process. You'll help people see the benefits of moving the process to the next level of performance.
- Describe how you will change the process in question, and how each person will be involved.
- Explain "what's in it for them" if they help to improve the process at hand. For example, "We'll all acquire more new customers and therefore get bigger bonuses."
- Identify and address the beliefs or assumptions that are driving resistance to the new process. For example, if a person says, "That new software won't work," ask, "What would it take for

you to think differently about this?" If he or she responds, "Well, I'd like proof that it worked in another company," provide the requested evidence.

- Have resisters listen to or participate in process benchmarking interviews, in which process improvement team members interview members of another organization that has had success with processes similar to the redesigned one your team has devised.

Rolling out the new business process

When you're ready to implement the new process, follow these steps:

1. **Communicate.** Get the message out about the upcoming implementation of the new process. Give everyone—managers, employees, and other people involved in the process—time to understand or reaffirm why the new process is needed, what it is, how things will be different and better, who was involved in the project, and what will happen when the new process becomes part of everyday operations. In most cases, you cannot overcommunicate this information.

2. **Educate and familiarize.** Build a more detailed understanding of how the new process works through role-play, practice, and simulation. Just as you used these techniques during phase three (redesigning the problematic process), you can use them now to test (or to demonstrate) how well the new process works. For instance, if you decide to practice the new process,

ask everyone who will be working in that process to try it out exactly as it's meant to unfold. During the practice, watch for problems, and then decide how to eliminate them.

3. **Pilot (if necessary).** If you suspect that some difficulties in the new process may still need to be worked out, pilot it. During a pilot, you run the new process as you would under actual business circumstances, but you limit its scope. For example, you might try the new process with just one group of customers, one sales region, or one product category. You can also constrain the pilot by time—for instance, by running it for several months and then assessing its effectiveness. Pilots are riskier than role-play, practice, and simulation, because they involve actual customers, products, or services. However, if you monitor pilots closely, you can fix problems as soon as they occur—while gaining valuable feedback that will help improve the process. One other advantage of using pilots is that the people participating in the pilot will be able help train others when you roll the new process out to other regions, products, and customer groups. Pilots also give skeptics the opportunity to observe the new process in action—and to reassure themselves that it is effective.

4. **Implement.** Put the new process into production by declaring the start of new operations. Begin to gather data on the new performance measures related to the process, and be available to answer questions and support people as they change the way they work. Recognize that there will be a learning curve and that people will need time to get the process right.

5. **Break from the past.** Remove the artifacts of the old process to reduce any temptation to shift back into previous habits. These artifacts may include old forms, paper stock, equipment, signage, and so forth. Removing these items sends a clear message that the new process is here to stay.

Phase 6: Continually Improve Your Business Process

ou've implemented the new process. Now you face another challenge: ensuring that the redesigned process continues to deliver the results you want. You now need to establish a system for continually monitoring—and improving—the redesigned process's performance. That means identifying and fixing problems as they come up.

To continually improve your process, you:

- Measure process performance according to the metrics you've chosen.

- Identify problems and take needed action.

- Update performance metrics and targets as necessary.

Measure the business process's performance

In your redesign phase (phase 3), you established metrics for measuring your new process's performance. You'll use those metrics to monitor the new process and make changes as needed to continually improve it.

The table "Metrics, Targets, and Data" highlights examples of the metric types you may be working with. It also provides examples of metrics, targets, and types of performance data gathered.

As the process owner, you should regularly "walk the process" to assess its performance—chatting with people who work in the

TABLE 5

Metrics, targets, and data

Metric type	Example	Possible target	Data and source
Quality: Is the new process's outcome free of errors or defects?	For a redesigned process intended to make a piece of equipment more reliable, a metric may be: number of break-downs per month.	No more than two breakdowns per month.	Monthly break-down reports from manufacturing personnel.
Cycle time: Does the process produce its intended outcome in a timely manner?	For a new process intended to speed up hiring, one metric might be: number of weeks to fill open position.	No more than four weeks to fill position.	Information on timeliness from hiring managers after each position is filled.
Customer satisfaction: Are customers satisfied with the process's outcome?	For a new process intended to improve customers' experience with your team, a metric might be: number of times customer calls service department before their problem is resolved.	One phone call needed to resolve customer problem.	Customer satisfaction survey results; call center records.
Cost: Does the process produce its intended outcome in a cost-effective manner?	For a redesigned process intended to improve the return on investments in consulting services, one metric might be: amount spent per quarter on consultants.	Between $15,000 and $20,000 spent on consultants per month.	Monthly expense reports from managers who use consultants

TABLE 6

Joe's dashboard

Metric	Target	Actual performance	Comment
Average time to complete a loan application.	24 hours from receipt of a completed application.	36 hours on average.	The underwriting department continues to reject loans due to incomplete documentation.
Percentage of complete applications received.	80% of initial applications include all documentation needed to process the loan.	69% of initial applications include all documentation needed to process the loan.	Loan officers are not providing the documentation checklist on all occasions.
Average number of open customer questions.	Zero: All customer questions are answered at the time they are received.	150 open customer questions.	The number is declining from an average of 300 open calls per month.

process, observing individual tasks, and checking adherence to procedures.

You should also maintain a "dashboard"—or graphical representation—showing the metrics used to track the process's performance, as well as the data indicating actual performance against targets. By prominently displaying this dashboard, you ensure that everyone who works in the process is continually aware of how it's performing. The table "Joe's Dashboard" shows examples.

Take needed action to improve performance

If the process's performance falls short of targets, you and your BPI team must decide what, if any, actions are needed to address the shortfalls. In some cases, you may decide not to take action. For example, Joe opts not to do anything different to address the 150 open customer questions at this point. That's because the number is declining from an average of 300, and he expects it to eventually move toward zero as the process continues to operate.

With other performance shortfalls, you may decide that action is required. For instance, Joe's BPI team determines to make some changes in how the loan officers work so that the percentage of complete applications received moves closer to the targeted 80 percent.

When team members explore ideas for actions that might further improve the process, ensure that they submit their ideas to the process owner rather than trying to make changes themselves. The process owner is best suited to evaluate particular changes, since he or she will consider the possible impact on other processes and departments—and keep "the big picture" in mind.

Revise performance metrics and targets as needed

As time passes, new business circumstances may suggest the need to revise the performance metrics and targets you've established for your redesigned process. For example, as competition in the financial services industry intensifies, Joe's BPI team determines that a target of "80 percent of initial applications include all documentation needed to process the loan" is not high enough to maintain the company's competitive edge. The team decides to raise the target performance to 95 percent.

As you might have concluded by now, BPI takes patience and discipline. But the benefits are well worth the effort. By continually honing the business processes in your work unit, you generate new efficiencies, improve productivity, and cut costs—all of which benefit your group *and* your company overall.

Tips and Tools

Tools for Improving Your Business Processes

Deciding Whether Process Improvement Is Necessary

The questions below relate to the signs and symptoms suggesting that your team may need to embark on a business process improvement (BPI) effort. Use this tool to decide whether to launch a BPI initiative.

Question:	Yes	No
1. Is your team failing to meet quality, cost, or time requirements?		
2. Are there significant external developments (for example, in customer preferences, competitors' behavior, and technology) that may require considerable adjustments to current processes?		
3. Are there important changes within your organization (for instance, a new corporate strategy emphasizing high-quality customer service) that may suggest the need for process improvement?		
4. Have you seen evidence of fragmentation and lack of cooperation or coherence in how work is being carried out?		
5. Are customers complaining about the quality of service they are getting from your team?		
6. Does your team's performance compare unfavorably with that of other teams in the organization that do similar work?		
7. Are employees expressing frustration with their job responsibilities?		
8. Do tasks often get done incorrectly the first time?		
9. Are some tasks taking too long to complete?		
10. Do certain procedures seem overly complicated; for example, multiple signoffs being required to approve a single purchase order?		
TOTALS		

*If you answered "**yes**" to most of these questions, your team probably needs to launch a BPI initiative.*

Planning a Process Redesign

If you've decided that a process redesign effort is necessary in your team,
use this worksheet to plan the initiative.

1. What process do you think would benefit from being redesigned?

2. What are the conditions or issues that prompted the launch of an improvement effort for this process? Why is this redesign necessary?

3. What do you see as the scope of this business process improvement (BPI) effort—that is, what will and won't be included?

4. What are the goals of the BPI effort?

5. How will you know that the BPI effort has succeeded?

6. Who will make up your BPI team? Indicate who will fill the following roles:

Project manager:
Process owner:
Process users:
Skeptics:
Facilitator:
Technology expert:

7. From which individuals in your organization—for example, your supervisor, peer managers, or heads of other functions—will your BPI team need support in order to carry out its work? List these individuals below. Next to each name, indicate the kind of support your team will need from that person. Examples may include approval for funding, ideas for redesigning the process, and participation in a practice or pilot for the redesigned process.

8. How will you ensure that your BPI team receives the support it needs from the individuals you identified in question 7?

9. What timetable do you anticipate for this BPI effort? List major milestones below, such as "analyzing the current process," "redesigning the process," "acquiring resources," and "implementing the new process." Next to each major milestone, indicate when you expect your team to reach that milestone.

10. What potential obstacles might your BPI team face as it carries out the BPI initiative? List the obstacles below, and indicate how you plan to surmount each one.

Creating a Functional Activity Flowchart

The worksheet below enables you to create a functional activity flowchart of a process. To create the flowchart, list the job titles of the people involved in the process on the left. For each job title in the chart, insert a box containing a short phrase representing what that person does at each step in the process. Insert diamonds containing a short phrase representing decisions people must make while carrying out the process. Number each box and diamond to indicate the sequence in which these activities and decisions are carried out.

Job title	

Process Report Card

This worksheet enables you to create a report card communicating customers' views of the quality of a current process that affects them and that you want to redesign. For each customer requirement for the process, describe what ideal, or "A," performance looks like, then indicate how customers would grade the process's current performance on that requirement.

Process to be redesigned:

Customer requirements *Example: Fast turnaround.*	What "A" performance looks like *Example: Order turned in within four hours or fewer.*	"Grade" by customer *Example: C+*

Process Benchmarking

This worksheet helps you develop a plan for benchmarking a process you want to redesign.

Process to be redesigned: _____

1. **Identify information benchmarking sources.**
   List sources that would be helpful for gathering information on which companies to use as benchmarks. Examples may include consultants specializing in benchmarking, industry trade associations, former employees of competitors, companies' published documents, and competitors' customers and suppliers. For each source you've identified, indicate who will contact that source and when.

Source	Who will contact	When

2. **Identify direct competitors to benchmark.**
   List companies that compete with yours and that perform the same process you want to improve.

3. **Identify noncompetitors to benchmark.**
   List companies that do not compete with yours but that perform the same process you want to improve.

4. **Identify world-class organizations to benchmark.**
   List companies that are considered "world-class" in the process you want to improve.

5. **Create benchmarking teams.**
   For each of the three types of benchmark targets you identified in steps 2–4, list members of your business process improvement (BPI) team who will be responsible for contacting those organizations.

   Competitor benchmarking team:

   Noncompetitor benchmarking team:

   World-class organizations benchmarking team:

6. **Prepare a list of benchmarking interview questions.**
   List the questions you want to ask each organization during your benchmarking interviews.

7. **Prepare a benchmarking interview script.**
   Fill in the information in the script below to customize it for the process you are trying to improve. Have BPI team members practice reading and responding to the script before conducting actual benchmarking interviews.

   - "Hello, my name is _____. I'm part of a team at _____."
   - "We're doing an analysis of our _____ process, and we understand that your organization is doing some interesting things in that area."
   - "Are you the person I should speak with regarding this process? If not, whom would you recommend I contact?"
   - "Is this a good time to talk? If not, when is a better time?"
   - "I have a list of questions that should take _____ minutes to answer."
   - "We'll be sharing our findings with participating organizations. Would you like a summary of our findings?"

- "Are you ready to answer the questions? The first is _____. The next question is _____." [State the remaining questions.]
- "Is it okay to call you back if we need to clarify some things?"
- "Thank you for your time."

Test Yourself

This section offers ten multiple-choice questions to help you identify your baseline knowledge of the essentials of business process improvement.

Answers to the questions are given at the end of the test.

1. A business process consists of three components. Two of them are inputs and activities. What is the third component called?

a. Products.

b. Outputs.

c. Artifacts.

2. A business process can be thought of as a series of events that bring together three elements in ways that create valuable outcomes. Two of those elements are people and technology. What is the third element?

a. Information.

b. Equipment.

c. Funding.

3. Which of the following is *not* something that would likely trigger a business process improvement (BPI) effort?

    a. Problematic performance in a team.

    b. A major shift in customer preferences.

    c. The hiring of a new manager in a department.

4. What is the third phase of a BPI effort?

    a. Redesign the existing process.

    b. Analyze the existing process.

    c. Acquire resources needed to implement the new process.

5. Maria is assembling a team to carry out a major business process improvement project. She has selected a project manager and process owner, as well as several individuals who work directly in the process that will be improved. She has also identified a facilitator and technology expert to serve on the team. Whom has she left out?

    a. A person who will take responsibility for ensuring that the project achieves its goals.

    b. Someone to track the improved process's performance.

    c. Several individuals who will stimulate productive debate about how to redesign the process.

6. You've created an "as is" flowchart for a process you want to improve. The chart shows all the steps in the process, along with the job titles of the people who carry out those steps. What type of flowchart have you created?

    a. Macro.

    b. Functional activity.

    c. Diamond.

7. Tom and his BPI team are brainstorming ways to improve a process. They've explored two questions: "How might we cut costs associated with this process?" and "Are there changes we could make to reduce the process's cycle time?" What other question should they be sure to ask themselves in order to envision a better process?

    a. "How might we improve the process to make it easier for customers to do business with us?"

    b. "Would the potential changes we're exploring require too many organizational changes?"

    c. "Which individuals carry out which steps in our current process?"

8. As the director of operations, you're working on a BPI effort with a large scope. In addition to the human resources and information technology departments, which additional function will you most likely need to collaborate with in order to get the resources you need to implement your new process?

    a. Finance.

    b. Marketing.

    c. Sales.

9. You've decided to redesign a process in ways that you expect might trigger resistance from some employees. Which of the following would *not* help you overcome that resistance?

   a. Point out how the new process will solve problems created by the old process.

   b. Clearly explain how people were operating incorrectly in the old process.

   c. Show employees how they will benefit from adopting the new process.

10. At one stage in a business process improvement effort, the process owner creates a "dashboard." What is the purpose of the dashboard?

   a. To help the BPI team decide which of several processes would benefit the most from improvement.

   b. To track how well a redesigned process is generating the desired results.

   c. To indicate the direction in which work will flow in a redesigned process.

Answers to test questions

1, b. Inputs start a process, and activities transform those inputs into outputs. For example, inputs for the process of building a house would include lumber, cement, and other materials. Activities would include digging the foundation and raising the walls. And the output would be the finished house.

2, a. People, technology, and information interact in business processes. For example, people carry out the activities that transform the process's inputs into outputs. Technology can facilitate process activities, such as when a person e-mails a customer or retrieves customer data from a database. And information can be a process input (such as the number of parts in a warehouse) or an output (for instance, a consultant's report). Information is all around people who work in a process—stored in a database, provided by a customer, or held in a person's mind.

3, c. While a newly hired manager may want to eventually improve one or more processes in his or her department, this is not an event that typically triggers a business process improvement effort. More likely triggers are inefficiencies or declining performance in a team, department, or organization, as well as major changes in the business landscape (such as significant shifts in customer preferences, the emergence of new competitors, and the advent of new technologies).

4, a. A BPI effort consists of six phases: (1) Plan: select a process to improve, (2) Analyze: examine the selected process, (3) Redesign: determine what changes you want to make to the target process, (4) Acquire resources: obtain the personnel, equipment, and other resources needed to make the process changes you've identified, (5) Implement: carry out the process changes, and (6) Continually improve: constantly evaluate the new process's effectiveness and make further changes as needed.

5, c. In addition to the team members Maria has already chosen, she should also select one or more skeptics—people who will challenge the design process and thus stimulate productive debate over ideas.

6, b. A functional activity "as is" flowchart depicts the more detailed steps in a process. It also shows the job titles of the people working in the process and the activities performed by each individual. A functional activity flowchart enables you to examine each component of the process and identify points where the process experiences delays or other problems.

7, a. In addition to asking questions about costs and cycle time, asking how you might make customers happier by changing the process can help you and your BPI team generate valuable ideas for redesigning the process. To explore this question, encourage members of your BPI team to envision a better process from the perspective of your customer—asking what customers might want from the process in terms of accuracy, convenience, and other forms of value.

8, a. With large-scope process changes, you will likely need to work closely with the HR, IT, and finance groups to obtain resources needed for implementing the new process. For example, perhaps you'll need the HR group to design a program for training people in the new process. You may want the IT group to help you install any new technology required by the redesigned process. And you may have to present a compelling business case for your new process to the finance department to receive funding for implementation of the process.

9, b. By explaining how people were operating incorrectly in the old process, you would likely make employees defensive, thereby intensifying their resistance. To overcome resistance, it's better to point out how the new process will solve problems created by the old process and to show employees how they will benefit from adopting the new process.

10, b. The purpose of a process dashboard is to highlight how well a redesigned process is working. A process dashboard contains information such as the performance metrics established for the redesigned process, the targeted performance for each metric, and the process's actual performance on each metric.

The process owner and others use this information to determine whether additional changes are needed to further improve the process. For example, suppose the BPI team has set a target of "All customer questions answered with one phone call," but the process dashboard shows that, on average, five phone calls are required to resolve customers' questions. In this case, the team will likely want to refine the new process so that it delivers results closer to targeted goals.

To Learn More

Articles

Davenport, Thomas H. "The Coming Commoditization of Processes." *Harvard Business Review*, June 2005.

As companies analyze, standardize, and quality-check business processes ranging from product development to CEO hiring, those processes will become commoditized—leading to a wave of business process outsourcing. Davenport explores this development. As he explains, a broad set of process standards will soon make it easy to determine whether a business capability can be improved by outsourcing it. Such standards will also help businesses compare service providers and evaluate the costs versus the benefits of process outsourcing. Eventually these costs and benefits will be so visible to buyers that outsourced processes will become a commodity, and prices will drop significantly. The low costs and low risk of outsourcing will accelerate the flow of jobs offshore, force companies to reassess their strategies, and change the basis of competition. The speed with which some businesses have already adopted process standards suggests that many previously unscrutinized areas are ripe for change.

Hall, Joseph M. and M. Eric Johnson. "When Should a Process Be Art, Not Science?" *Harvard Business Review*, March 2009.

Managers have gone overboard with process standardization. Many processes—such as leadership training or auditing—are more art than science. Imposing rigid rules on them squashes innovation, reduces accountability, and harms performance. The authors advise companies to rescue artistic processes from the tide of standardization with a three-step approach that begins with identifying what should and shouldn't be art.

Hammer, Michael. "Deep Change: How Operational Innovation Can Transform Your Company." *Harvard Business Review* On-Point Enhanced Edition. Boston: Harvard Business School Publishing, 2004.

Breakthrough operational innovations can destroy competitors and shake up entire industries. Just look at Dell, Toyota, and Wal-Mart. This article offers practical advice on how to develop operational innovations, such as looking for role models outside your industry to emulate and identifying—and then defying—constraining assumptions about how work should be done. The author also discusses the best way to implement operational innovations. For instance, because they are disruptive by nature, operational-innovation projects should be concentrated in those activities with the greatest impact on enterprise strategic goals. Operational innovation may feel unglamorous or unfamiliar to many executives, but it is the only lasting basis for superior performance.

Hammer, Michael. "Process Audit." *Harvard Business Review*, April 2007.

Few executives question the idea that by redesigning business processes they can achieve extraordinary improvements in cost, quality, speed, and profitability. Yet in spite of their intentions and investments, many executives flounder, unsure about what exactly needs to be changed, by how much, and when. As a result, many organizations make little progress—if any at all—in their attempts to transform business processes. The author spent five years working with a group of leading companies to develop the Process and Enterprise Maturity Model (PEMM), a framework that helps executives comprehend, formulate, and assess process-based transformation efforts. PEMM is different from other frameworks because it applies to all industries and all processes.

Puryear, Rudy and Christine Detrick. "Are You Sending Your Problems Offshore?" *Harvard Management Update*, February 2006.

It seems straightforward enough—why not simply outsource routine financial reporting functions offshore? Sure, you'll save some money. But if these processes are flawed to begin with, you only transplant their inefficiencies elsewhere, missing the greater opportunity to streamline. The authors contend that while outsourcing can play a central role in an effort to improve operations, a significant chunk of any program's benefits comes from changing attitudes, behaviors, and cultures within the company's own walls.

Books

Harmon, Paul. *Business Process Change: A Manager's Guide to Improving, Redesigning, and Automating Processes.* San Francisco: Morgan Kaufmann, 2003.

Every company wants to improve the way it does business, and your process redesign efforts can help your organization reach that goal. Harmon describes a variety of business process change techniques. He discusses the process change problems facing today's managers, summarizes the state-of-the-art business process analysis and improvement methods available, and presents a methodology based on best practices that can be tailored to specific needs and that acknowledges the human aspects of process redesign. Detailed case studies show what these methods look like in action.

Jacka, J. Mike and Paulette J. Keller. *Business Process Mapping: Improving Customer Satisfaction*, 2nd ed. Hoboken, New Jersey: John Wiley & Sons, 2009.

The authors cut through the drudgery of process mapping with a path-breaking approach that enables the reader to better understand processes, how they function, and how they work together toward the successful achievement of business objectives. This book offers a different way of thinking and new tools to assist you in process analysis and improvement. The authors use real-life examples and anecdotes, and each chapter includes a "Recap" and "Key Analysis Points" that highlight the chapter's key takeaways.

Keen, Peter and Mark McDonald. *The eProcess Edge: Creating Customer Value in the Internet Economy*. New York: McGraw-Hill, 2000.

This book provides a practical roadmap that shows managers and technology decision-makers exactly how to improve processes and capabilities, gain a competitive advantage through relationships, and help their companies prosper. The eProcess model allows companies to drive faster revenue growth and reap greater profits by combining new technology with business processes and by building stronger relationships that generate repeat business.

Madison, Dan. *Process Mapping, Process Improvement, and Process Management*. Chico, CA: Paton Press, 2005.

This simple, well-written survey of process redesign presents the evolution of process focused work management styles. It introduces the tools of process mapping, identifies the roles and responsibilities of individuals who participate in process improvement efforts, and presents a ten-step redesign methodology. The author also explains the process design principles that enable you to custom-fit his methodology to your own challenges. Additional chapters by other authors discuss cross-department process management and the use of computer simulation in process redesign.

Teaching Note

Marshall, Paul W. "A Note on Process Analysis." Harvard Business School Case No. 9-675-038. Boston: Harvard Business School Publishing, rev. July 1, 1979.

Marshall defines business processes, provides examples, and explains the nature of inputs, outputs, and tasks that make up processes. He also introduces the four characteristics of a process: capacity, efficiency, effectiveness, and flexibility. In addition, Marshall provides a sample process flowchart and explains how to analyze an existing process that you are considering improving.

Sources for Improving Business Processes

The following sources aided in development of this book:

Gebelein, Susan H., Kristie J. Nelson-Neuhaus, Carol J. Skube, David G. Lee, Lisa A. Stevens, Lowell W. Hellervik, and Brian L. Davis. *Successful Manager's Handbook,* 7th ed. Minneapolis, MN: Personnel Decisions International, 2004.

Harmon, Paul. *Business Process Change: A Manager's Guide to Improving, Redesigning, and Automating Processes.* San Francisco: Morgan Kaufmann, 2003.

http://searchcio.techtarget.com/sDefinition/0,,sid19_gci536451,00.html

http://www.induction.to/six-sigma/tsld005.htm

Madison, Dan. *Process Mapping, Process Improvement, and Process Management.* Chico, CA: Paton Press, 2005.

Marshall, Paul W. "A Note on Process Analysis." Harvard Business School Note 9-675-038, rev. July 1, 1979.

Notes

How to Order

Harvard Business School Press publications are available world-wide from your local bookseller or online retailer.

You can also call:
1-800-668-6780

Our product consultants are available to help you 8:00 a.m.–6:00 p.m., Monday–Friday, Eastern Time. Outside the U.S. and Canada, call: 617-783-7450.

Please call about special discounts for quantities greater than ten.

You can order online at:
www.HBSPress.org

Printed in the USA
CPSIA information can be obtained
at www.ICGtesting.com
LVHW021051041223
765479LV00005B/637

9 781422 129739